D1118688

WITHDRAWN

Dear Parent:
Your child's love of reading starts here!

Every child learns to read in a different way and at his or her own speed. Some go back and forth between reading levels and read favorite books again and again. Others read through each level in order. You can help your young reader improve and become more confident by encouraging his or her own interests and abilities. From books your child reads with you to the first books he or she reads alone, there are I Can Read Books for every stage of reading:

SHARED READING
Basic language, word repetition, and whimsical illustrations, ideal for sharing with your emergent reader

BEGINNING READING
Short sentences, familiar words, and simple concepts for children eager to read on their own

READING WITH HELP
Engaging stories, longer sentences, and language play for developing readers

READING ALONE
Complex plots, challenging vocabulary, and high-interest topics for the independent reader

I Can Read Books have introduced children to the joy of reading since 1957. Featuring award-winning authors and illustrators and a fabulous cast of beloved characters, I Can Read Books set the standard for beginning readers.

A lifetime of discovery begins with the magical words "I Can Read!"

Visit www.icanread.com for information
on enriching your child's reading experience.

Visit www.zonderkidz.com/icanread for more faith-based
I Can Read! titles from Zonderkidz.

ZONDERKIDZ

Fiona's Train Ride
Copyright © 2022 by Zondervan
Illustrations © 2022 by Zondervan

An **I Can Read Book**

Requests for information should be addressed to:
Zonderkidz, 3900 *Sparks Drive SE, Grand Rapids, Michigan* 49546

Softcover ISBN 978-0-310-76311-6
Hardcover ISBN 978-0-310-76329-1
Ebook ISBN 978-0-310-76607-0

Any internet addresses (websites, blogs, etc.) and telephone numbers in this book are offered as a resource. They are not intended in any way to be or imply an endorsement by Zondervan, nor does Zondervan vouch for the content of these sites and numbers for the life of this book.

No part of this publication may be reproduced, stored in a retrieval system, or transmitted in any form or by any means — electronic, mechanical, photocopy, recording, or any other — except for brief quotations in printed reviews, without the prior permission of the publisher.

Zonderkidz is a trademark of Zondervan.

Art direction and design: Diane Mielke
Content Contributor: Barbara Herndon

I Can Read® and I Can Read Book® are trademarks of HarperCollins Publishers.

Printed in United States of America

22 23 24 25 26 27 /LSCC/ 15 14 13 12 11 10 9 8 7 6 5 4 3 2 1

ZONDERkidz · 1 BEGINNING READING · I Can Read!

Fiona's Train Ride

New York Times **Bestselling Illustrator**
Richard Cowdrey
with Donald Wu

ZONDERkidz

Fiona was happy! She and
Mama were eating lunch.
"Good news, Mama," said
Fiona. "A red panda baby
was born! Can I go see her?"

Mama munched her squash.

Fiona grabbed lettuce.

"Babies need rest," said Mama.

"Wait until later."

Later that day, Fiona told her
friends, "Did you hear?
A red panda baby was born.
We should go see her."

"That is a long walk," said tortoise.

"It is up lots of hills.

It is down lots of hills," said skunk.

"I'm too tired," said sloth.

As the animals thought about
the baby, they heard something.
"CHOO-CHOO! CHUG-CHUG!
DING, DING, DING!!"

It was the zoo train.

Fiona saw the train.
It looked fun. It looked fast.
She wanted to ride on
that train!

Fiona asked her friends,
"Have you been on the train?"

The cardinal bird said,

"I rode on top once."

"I rode with the zookeeper once,"

said skunk.

Fiona wanted to go on the train.

She had an idea!

"Let's ride the train

to go see the new baby."

When the zoo closed,
Fiona and her friends
went to find the train.
They saw a sign.
It said: "Train Stop Ahead."

"There it is!" said skunk.

"Who will drive?" asked sloth,

as he hung from the roof.

Fiona got in the front car.

"I will drive," said Fiona.

"I've got this!"

But Fiona was stuck.

She could not turn around.

How could she see?

How could she steer?

Just then, the monkeys ran up.

"Fiona, do you need help?"

they asked.

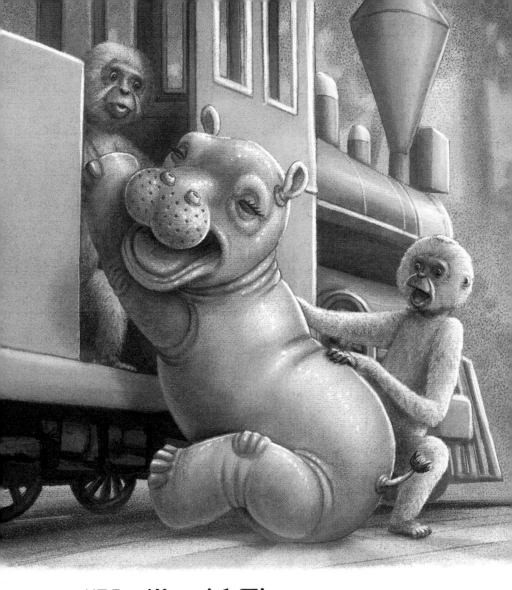

"Yes!" said Fiona.

The monkeys pushed.

The monkeys pulled.

Fiona came tumbling out.

19

"Let's try again," said Fiona.
This time the monkeys
helped her get in.

Fiona was in the first train car.

She was driving the train!

DING, DING, DING the bell rang.

CHOO-CHOO! CHUG-CHUG!

The train started to move.

CHOO-CHOO!

CHUG-CHUG!

Fiona drove the train

to see the new baby.

"We are here!" said Fiona.
The animals got out
of the train.
They peeked at the new baby.

The baby red panda
was very cute and sleepy.
"She is fuzzy!"
"She really is red!"
"She looks just like her mama!"

After the animals whispered hello,
they got back on the train.

CHOO-CHOO!

CHUG-CHUG!

Fiona drove the train
back to the train stop.

All the animal friends
tumbled out of the train.
It was time to go home.

"You are a good train driver,
Fiona," said skunk.

"Let's go again," said sloth.

"Maybe tomorrow," yawned
Fiona. She was sleepy.

"Did you see the new
baby red panda?"
asked Mama.

"Yes," said Fiona.
"She is very cute.
And very sleepy."

Fiona was sleepy too.